BATTLE CRY!

Write a Soldier's Adventure
Ten Days of Battle

By

Jan May

Battle Cry by Jan May
Copyright, Jan May, 2017

Education and Language Arts

All rights reserved. No part of this book may be used or reproduced in any manner, whatsoever, without written permission, except where noted in text.

Printed in the United States of America
First Edition. Print Edition, 2018

 Clip Art by Doodle Dad Designs https ://www.teacherspayteachers.com/Store/Doodle-Dad-Designs

Published by New Millennium Girl Books
www.NewMillenniumGirlBooks.com

TABLE OF CONTENTS

LESSON ONE:
Creating a Soldier Character — 7

LESSON TWO:
Using your Senses to Develop a Setting — 18

LESSON THREE:
Plotting a Battle Plan — 24

LESSON FOUR:
Using Comic Relief — 41

LESSON FIVE:
Onomatopoeia and Interjections — 45

LESSON SIX:
Figurative Language -Personification — 50

LESSON SEVEN:
Figurative Language-Similes — 55

LESSON EIGHT:
Show Don't Tell — 61

LESSON NINE:
Get the Most out of Your Dialogue — 64

LESSON TEN:
Add an Adjective — 68

LESSON ELEVEN:
Vivid Verbs — 73

LESSON TWELVE:
Editing — 77

PUTTING IT ALL TOGETHER: — 78

ABOUT THE AUTHOR — 101

THIS BOOK IS DEDICATED

TO MY SON DANIEL WHO LOVED PLAYING

TOY SOLDIERS FOR HOURS ON END

AND TO MY SOLDIER SON IN THE FAITH, JUDAH

AND TO ALL THE BRAVE MEN AND WOMEN WHO

FIGHT TO DEFEND OUR FREEDOM

MAY GOD'S PROTECTION BE OVER ALL

WHAT'S IT ALL ABOUT?

"David became more and more powerful, because the Lord Almighty was with him."
                                          I Chronicles 11:9

God has a wonderful plan for the mixture of constant motion and conquering spirit residing in boys. George Washington was a great example of this. He fought many mock battles on the play ground during his schooldays as a boy and would beg the headmaster to give him and his classmates more time to finish the skirmish after lunch. He became the Father of our Country and the Father of Freedom around the world!

My prayer is that this book will encourage boys to be young men full of courage and valor, ready to tackle every challenge bravely. To protect with honor, the people and property God has given them on God's behalf and His kingdom. We need brave, strong, conquering boys!

This curriculum is designed to be boy friendly with twelve easy self-guided step-by-step lessons walking the student through the basics of creative writing in character, setting, and plot development. Each lesson includes: Writing Time, Battle Craft Time or a Battle Activity. Role-playing is monumental in building inspiration for writing so included are creative activities such as building a fort and a Boot Camp obstacle course. There also will be time spent on illustrating and map making which will be assembled along with the written pages at the end of this course into a book.

As a creative writing teacher, I am constantly barraged by boys to write a curriculum so that they can write battle stories. They remind me of a fiery shepherd boy full of faith, who chose five smooth stones to slay the giant, Goliath. God had His hand on David to become a mighty warrior on and off the battlefield. The Bible says that David fulfilled all God's will in His generation. May the Lord do the same with your boys!

SUPPLY LIST FOR CRAFTS AND ACTIVITIES

- Homemade Clay: 2 cups flour, 1 cup salt, 4 t cream of tartar, 2 T oil
- Large shirt box for clay diorama (9 x 11)
- Acrylic paints (all colors) to paint clay diorama figures and acrylic paints in army greens, tan, and brown for tank marble painting
- Cotton balls for tree tops
- White paper to draw illustrations
- White paper to use in painting
- Camouflage colored construction paper for marble tank craft
- Marbles for marble painting and shirt box lid
- 2-4 lawn chairs for obstacle course
- 10 small plastic balls and bucket or target and Nerf gun for obstacle course
- Rope, timer and flag for obstacle course

LESSON 1
CREATE A SOLDIER CHARACTER

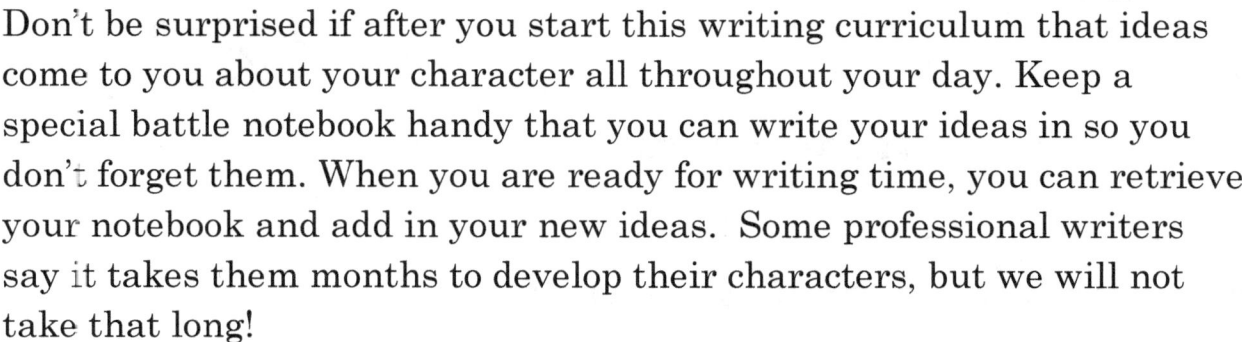

Your main character is called the protagonist. Developing him will take some time and thought. Don't be surprised if after you start this writing curriculum that ideas come to you about your character all throughout your day. Keep a special battle notebook handy that you can write your ideas in so you don't forget them. When you are ready for writing time, you can retrieve your notebook and add in your new ideas. Some professional writers say it takes them months to develop their characters, but we will not take that long!

A good story will help the protagonist to grow in character. In order to do this, give your characters weaknesses. If he starts out selfish, give him opportunities to be selfless. If he is fearful, give him a situation where he must face his fears to save someone else and be brave. Think about your own life and the lives of the people you know. That will give you ideas. Your characters can learn to trust God on the battlefield for protection, wisdom and strategy. Of all the places on earth, most soldiers rely on God's help once in combat. They realize He watches over all battles of all men.

CREATE A SOLDIER CHARACTER WORKSHEET

Your first assignment is to create your protagonist or main soldier character. Fill out the character worksheet below and on the next two pages.

1. **WHAT IS YOUR CHARACTER'S NAME?**
   _____

2. **DOES HE HAVE A BATTLEFIELD NICK NAME?**
   _____

3. **HOW OLD IS YOUR CHARACTER?** _____

4. **WHERE IS HE FROM? CITY, STATE, COUNTRY:**
   _____

5. **DESCRIBE WHAT HE LOOKS LIKE. DOES HE HAVE ANY SPECIAL FEATURES?**

   BIG EYES, NOSE, OR EARS, MISSING TEETH, SCARS, MUSTACHE OR BEARD, SQUINTY EYES, MUSCULAR ARMS, OR OTHER:
   _____
   _____
   _____

6. **WHICH DIVISION OF THE MILITARY IS HE IN? ARMY, NAVY, AIR FORCE, MARINES, NAVY SEALS, GREEN BERET, OR OTHER:**

   _____ **WHAT IS HIS RANK?** _____ SEE PAGE 100 FOR A LIST OF RANKS

7. WHAT IS HIS M.O.S. IN THE ARMY? M.O.S. MEANS MILITARY OCCUPATIONS SPECIALTY CODE (OR HIS JOB).

    INFANTRY-FOOT SOLDIER-GROUND POUNDER
    CALVARY-ARMORED TRUCK TRANSPORTER
    FIELD ARTILLERY CREW
    CAV SCOUT-COMMANDERS EYES AND EARS
    ENGINEER-BUILDER
    SIGNAL-COMMUNICATION OPERATOR
    INTELLIGENCE
    AMMUNITION SPECIALIST
    WATERCRAFT OPERATOR
    SPECIAL OPS FORCES
    SHARP SHOOTER
    PILOT
    MEDIC
    OTHER_____

8. CREATE A PERSONALITY: CHOOSE FROM THE LIST AND CREATE SOME OF YOUR OWN. CIRCLE THE ONES YOU LIKE:

				ADD YOUR OWN
FUNNY	STRONG	HAPPY	FEISTY	_____
LOUD	QUIET	SERIOUS	OUTGOING	_____
BRAVE	WITTY	GLARES	ENERGETIC	_____
SPUNKY	SILLY	SPORTY	HELPFUL	_____
PROUD	MEAN	HUMBLE	PLAYFUL	_____
SHY	SMILES	KIND	GENEROUS	_____

9. WHAT SPECIAL ABILITIES DOES HE HAVE?

    SHARP SHOOTER   ADD YOUR OWN
    QUICK PROBLEM SOLVER
    BUILDER   _____
    COMPUTER TECH   _____
    CANINE TRAINING   _____
    ELECTRICIAN   _____
    MECHANIC   _____
    MARCH LONG DISTANCES _____
    BRAVE LEADER   _____
    SPECIAL FORCES   _____
    CALM UNDER STRESS   _____
    HONEST CHARACTER   _____

CREATE BATTLE BUDDIES

Battle buddies are very important to every mission. Your character will want loyal men, who are well trained to be by his side in combat. To help him, let's create several battle buddies by filling out the lines below:

NAME _____
NICK NAME_____
AGE_____
RANK_____
SPECIAL FEATURES _____
MILITARY M.O.S. _____

NICK NAME_____
AGE_____
RANK_____
SPECIAL FEATURES _____
MILITARY M.O.S. _____

NAME _____
NICK NAME_____
AGE_____
RANK_____
SPECIAL FEATURES _____
MILITARY M.O.S. _____

BATTLE CRAFT TIME

Make an army folder to put your story pages, maps and illustrations in. There are several words and images on the next several pages. Cut out and color the ones you like then glue them onto a tan, green or black folder.

TOP SECRET

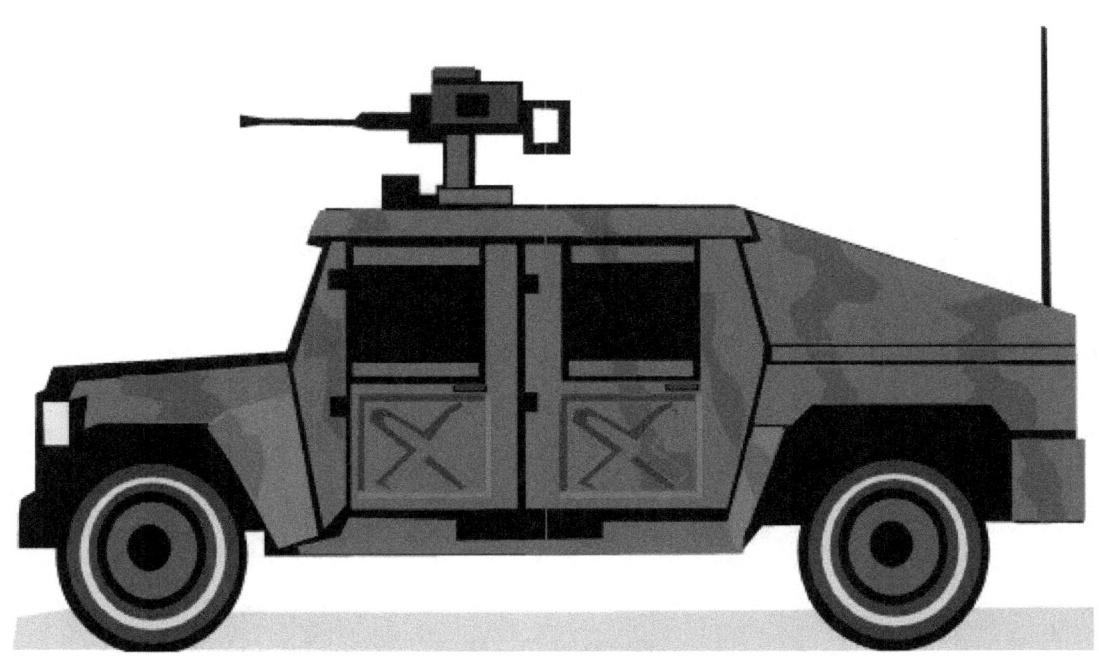

CUT OUT AND GLUE ONTO YOUR FOLDER

BATTLE BOOK

OPTIONAL - COLOR THE IMAGES

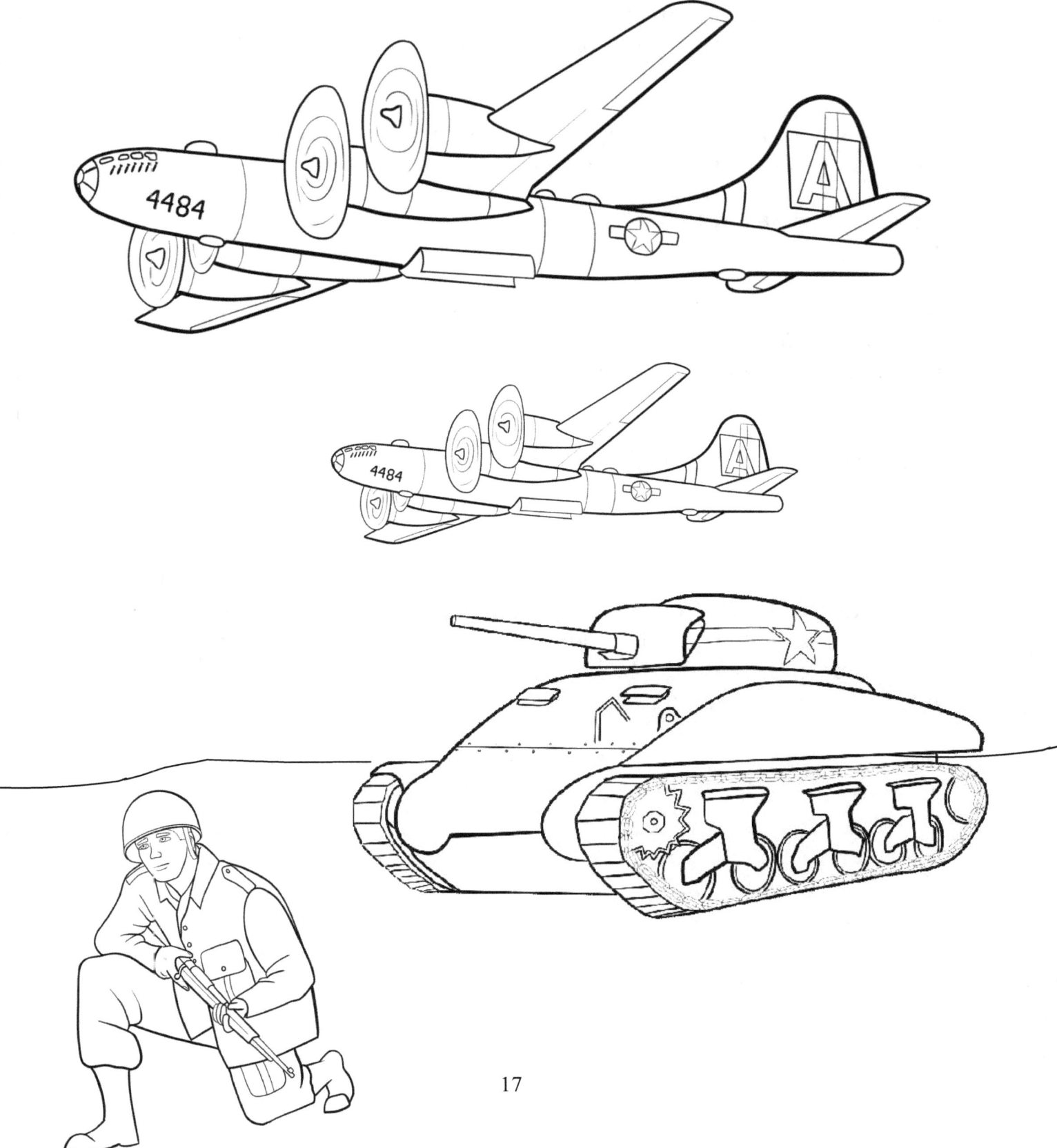

LESSON 2
CHOOSE YOUR SETTING

A setting is the location, surroundings and time in history where your story is taking place.

Choose a war or make one up of your own-this is not a complete list. (It can even be fantasy war!) Circle one:

REVOLUTIONARY WAR
CIVIL WAR
WWI
WWII
DESERT STORM
OPERATION ENDURING FREEDOM
OTHER _____

Is your mission in a city, dessert, rain forest, abandoned town, cave or other?
_____

Use your five senses to describe your battlefield. Use as many adjectives as you can to help you, like color or size. There are times a soldier may not be on the battlefield. Maybe he will be in a foxhole, vehicle or barracks. Add some description for those places too.

SIGHTS   **SOUNDS**
_____   _____
_____   _____
_____   _____
_____   _____
_____   _____

SMELLS

_____
_____
_____
_____
_____

TEXTURES
This is how something feels-for example, soft, rough, gooey, cold, smooth, etc.

_____
_____
_____
_____
_____

SOLDIERS EAT OUT OF PACKS CALLED MRE'S WHEN THEY ARE OUT ON A MISSION

An MRE is a **Meal, Ready-to-Eat** in a lightweight plastic package for soldiers to eat while they are away from base. Some packs contain chemical sources to heat the meal up. Some favorites of the soldiers are beef teriyaki and meatloaf with gravy!

Soldiers might also taste sand, grass, blood, salt, or dirt.

TASTES

_____
_____
_____
_____
_____

MILITARY PROPS

In a theatrical play special objects are used to make the scenes more realistic. If the play takes place in a school room, the objects may be books, a globe or a desk. If the play takes place at a beach, the objects may be a beach ball, sand shovel and beach chair. These objects are called props. This is the same in a written story. It needs props to make it sound more realistic. What special soldier items or objects could you add into your story as props? Here are some examples to get you started. Fill in the blanks below of more props.

HELMETS _____
PACKS _____
BOOTS _____
CAMOUFLAGE GEAR _____
WEAPONS _____
CANTEENS _____
RADIO COMMUNICATIONS _____

"BOOT CAMP"
B.C.T. - BASIC COMBAT TRAINING

It changes every soldier's life – Boot Camp! B.C.T. is usually for ten weeks; twelve hour days. It's hard, grueling work but it makes soldiers out of ordinary men molding them for the battle field. Every soldier starts out in B.C.T. where they are trained to handle the rigors of combat. They will:

Learn to trust their leadership
Learn how to take orders
Learn how to march in ranks
Learn team building and how to overcome obstacles
Learn how to handle weapons and artillery
Learn how to stay in top physical condition
Learn how to discipline their bodies to sleep less, eat less, and endure hardships
Learn battle strategies
Learn how to stay calm in difficult conditions
Learn basic first aid and combat life saving
Learn to adapt to hard situations and move on!

Many soldiers will give credit to their Boot Camp Drill Sergeant for their lives being saved during battle. The men that your character starts basic training with are the same guys he will be in combat with later.

LOOK ON PAGE 99 AND CHOOSE THE UNIT TYPE YOUR SOLDIER WILL BE WORKING IN.

WRITING TIME - Write a scene about your character's experience in B.C.T. If you need more writing pages, look in the back of this book.

BATTLE ACTIVITY
MAKE A BOOT CAMP OBSTACLE COURSE IN YOUR BACK YARD
TIME YOURSELF AND SEE HOW FAST YOU CAN MOVE THROUGH AND CAPTURE THE FLAG!

Many times soldiers have to help each other over hurdles. Invite a friend, brother or sister to join you. See whose time is the fastest or try to beat your own time. Think of the battle story you are writing as you go along.

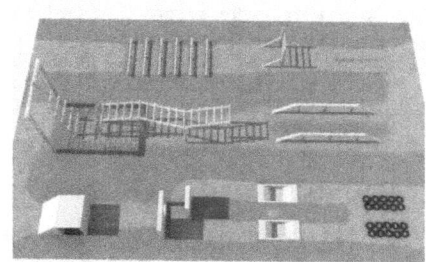

Read through all the instructions before you begin setting up to make sure you have all the items you need.

- Tie a **flag** or handkerchief near the beginning of the course
- Begin by hopping up with both feet 10 steps
- Crawl through **3-4 lawn chairs**
- Stand up and do 5 jumping jacks
- Lay a **rope** on the ground and hop with one foot on one side then another all the way down to the end of the rope.
- Lay on the ground and do 5 sit ups
- Stand up and throw **10 small plastic balls into a bucket** 5-7 feet away or **shoot a target**
- Do 5 more jumping jacks
- Run over to the lawn chairs and crawl back through to the other side
- Capture the flag!

LESSON 3
PLOTTING A BATTLE PLAN

A plot is like a road map of all the things that will happen in a story from beginning to end. You may not know exactly everything that will happen yet, but by writing out a plan it will give you more ideas and help your story stay organized. You can always add or make changes later.

Tension is a good thing in developing a plot. Like a roller coaster ride: First everything seems nice and calm, then *Bam!* You go around and around, twist upside down and you feel sick but excited. *Whoosh!* Add some twists and turns in your plot. Your character can't always succeed in his first try to overcome an obstacle. Your story might begin when your character goes to boot camp and then gets deployed (sent out on a mission). What is his first day like? Does he get along with everyone or not? Does he make friends? You can start out slow and let the battle tension grow.

Develop a Battle Plan. This is a rough outline only; you can write short phrases or abbreviate words. Use a pencil so you can add or take things out as you go along, so it doesn't have to be exact.

WRITING TIME: Fill in the plot handouts on the next several pages.

YOUR STORY WILL BE WRITTEN IN THREE SECTIONS: THE BEGINNING, MIDDLE AND END

The Beginning introduces your main character and the problem they face in battle. The first sentences should start the story off with **action** to draw the reader in. This is called a HOOK.

Practice Writing a Hook for your Story:
_____
_____
_____
_____
_____

FILL IN YOUR CHARACTER'S

TOP SECRET MISSION FILE

Who _____

What_____

Why_____

When_____

Where_____

EXTRA FILES FOR FUTURE MISSIONS

FILL IN YOUR CHARACTER'S

TOP SECRET MISSION FILE

Who _____

What_____

Why_____

When_____

Where_____

FILL IN YOUR CHARACTER'S

TOP SECRET MISSION FILE

Who _____

What_____

Why_____

When_____

Where_____

FILL OUT YOUR PLOT OUTLINE FOR THE BEGINNING OF YOUR STORY:

DAY 1- Introduce your main character, what is his life like before he goes into the military?

_____
_____
_____
_____
_____
_____

DAY 2 - Describe the BCT setting- What does he think about it? What is he doing? Is his squad getting ready to deploy (go on a mission)?

_____
_____
_____
_____
_____
_____

DAY 3 - What is his platoon's plan of action?

_____
_____
_____
_____
_____

The Middle of a story is where your character tries to solve the problem. It might even get worse. Think drama, drama, drama! Some writers use the one, two, three method: The first two attempts to solve the problem fail and on the third try, the character succeeds.

FILL OUT YOUR PLOT OUTLINE FOR THE MIDDLE OF THE STORY:

Write about the beginning of their mission and some of the problems they are facing:

DAY 4 - Battle begins - What is their goal- To take over an area? To blow up a bridge or enemy supplies? To secure an area? To rescue someone? To keep peace? Include weapons and artillery from the pages at the back of this book.

_____
_____
_____
_____
_____

DAY 5 - Give them a problem to overcome as the enemy advances:

_____
_____
_____
_____

DAY 6 - How do they overcome the attack?

_____
_____
_____
_____
_____

The Ending is where your soldier character overcomes his problem and grows in the process. Overcoming hardships makes a person stronger. If they start out fearful, they learn to trust God and be brave. If they start out selfish, they learn the honor of self sacrifice; if they lack confidence, they learn confidence through experience.

FILL OUT YOUR PLOT OUTLINE FOR THE ENDING OF THE STORY:

DAY 7 - Can you add a twist by making another problem crop up? What challenges are they facing?

_____
_____
_____
_____
_____
_____
_____

DAY 8 - How will the men react to the twist above?

_____
_____
_____
_____
_____
_____
_____

DAY 9 - Help them overcome the obstacles:
___
___
___
___
___
___
___

DAY 10 - The Ending is where your soldiers win the battle and come home as victors. So wrap up what's happening and come to a close.

___
___
___
___
___
___
___
___

BATTLE ACTIVITY

On the next several pages read about the U.S. Military's Alphabet. Create your own secret code with the sheets provided. Have fun practicing your code by sending messages to a brother, sister, parent or friend. Remember to give them a copy of your alphabet so they can decode your message!

SECRET CODES ARE USED IN BATTLES TO PASS IMPORTANT INFORMATION QUICKLY TO AND FROM THE BATTLEFIELD

*Below is the official U.S. Military Alphabet. Soldiers use this for correct pronunciation when talking over radios and communications. We will use it as a secret code. See if you can decode the messages below by using the key in the box: Answers on page 100.

```
A: Alpha      N: November
B: Bravo      O: Oscar
C: Charlie    P: Papa
D: Delta      Q: Quebec
E: Echo       R: Romeo
F: Foxtrot    S: Sierra
G: Golf       T: Tango
H: Hotel      U: Uniform
I: India      V: Victor
J: Juliet     W: Walrus
K: Kilo       X: X-Ray
L: Lima       Y: Yankee
M: Mike       Z: Zulu
```

Golf Echo Tango Papa India Zulu Zula Alpha
_____

Papa Lima Alpha Yankee Oscar Uniform Tango Sierra India Delta Echo
_____

Bravo Alpha Kilo Echo Charlie Oscar Oscar Kilo India Echo Sierra Walrus India Tango Hotel Mike Echo
_____

OPTIONAL – COLOR PICTURE

MAKE YOUR OWN MILITARY ALPHABET BELOW BY CHOOSING YOUR OWN WORDS TO REPRESENT EACH LETTER IN THE ALPHABET. CUT OUT YOUR CODE AND KEEP IT IN A SAFE PLACE TO DECODE MESSAGES.

MY SECRET CODE

A=_____

B=_____

C=_____

D=_____

E=_____

F=_____

G=_____

H=_____

I=_____

J=_____

K=_____

L=_____

M=_____

N=_____

O=_____

P=_____

Q=_____

R=_____

S=_____

T=_____

U=_____

V=_____

W=_____

X=_____

Y=_____

Z=_____

MAKE AN EXTRA COPY FOR A BROTHER, SISTER, FRIEND OR PARENT TO SEND MESSAGES TO.

MY SECRET CODE

A=_____ N=_____

B=_____ O=_____

C=_____ P=_____

D=_____ Q=_____

E=_____ R=_____

F=_____ S=_____

G=_____ T=_____

H=_____ U=_____

I=_____ V=_____

J=_____ W=_____

K=_____ X=_____

L=_____ Y=_____

M=_____ Z=_____

MAKE AN EXTRA COPY FOR A BROTHER, SISTER, FRIEND OR PARENT TO SEND MESSAGES TO.

MY SECRET CODE

A=_____

B=_____

C=_____

D=_____

E=_____

F=_____

G=_____

H=_____

I=_____

J=_____

K=_____

L=_____

M=_____

N=_____

O=_____

P=_____

Q=_____

R=_____

S=_____

T=_____

U=_____

V=_____

W=_____

X=_____

Y=_____

Z=_____

MAKE AN EXTRA COPY FOR A BROTHER, SISTER, FRIEND OR PARENT TO SEND MESSAGES TO.

MY SECRET CODE

A=_____   N=_____

B=_____   O=_____

C=_____   P=_____

D=_____   Q=_____

E=_____   R=_____

F=_____   S=_____

G=_____   T=_____

H=_____   U=_____

I=_____   V=_____

J=_____   W=_____

K=_____   X=_____

L=_____   Y=_____

M=_____   Z=_____

LESSON 4
THE BAD GUYS AND COMIC RELIEF

The bad guys in a story are called antagonists. They are trying to stop your character from reaching his goal. They help create conflict that makes a story interesting.

Who are your bad guys?

_____
_____

Why are they fighting against your army?

_____
_____

What are their strengths?

_____
_____

What are their weaknesses?

_____
_____

Do they have any special weapons or artillery?

_____
_____

COMIC RELIEF

Sometimes too much of battle scenes or intensity can be overwhelming, so the comic relief was invented. Most stories that are intense need a paragraph or two intertwined that are lighter hearted and even funny. They called this *Comic Relief* because it relieves the reader of intensity for a time so that they can continue engaging in the battle.

Think of a few things that can help bring comic relief along the way in your story. Below are some ideas to help you. Add some of your own ideas on the blank lines.

- A soldier is having a thought or dream about something pleasant from home
- Some soldiers prank other soldiers
- Soldiers get letters or packages from home that are fun
- Some soldier always likes to tell jokes
- The squad might play a sports game
- _____
- _____
- _____

WRITING TIME - Begin by writing several paragraphs of your story below using a good hook. Skip every other line so you can edit, change or add more things in later. Use your plot outline for day 1 for ideas.

BATTLE CRAFT TIME
DRAW A MAP OF THE BATTLE FIELD

- On a plain sheet of white paper draw a map of the battlefield.
- Draw the surroundings, buildings, trees, vehicles, bridges, rivers, etc.
- Draw where your soldiers are camped.
- Draw where the enemy is camped.
- Draw where each army's artillery is. Look at pages in the back for ideas.
- Color your map and save it in your battle folder as an illustration to use at the end of this book when you put your story all together.

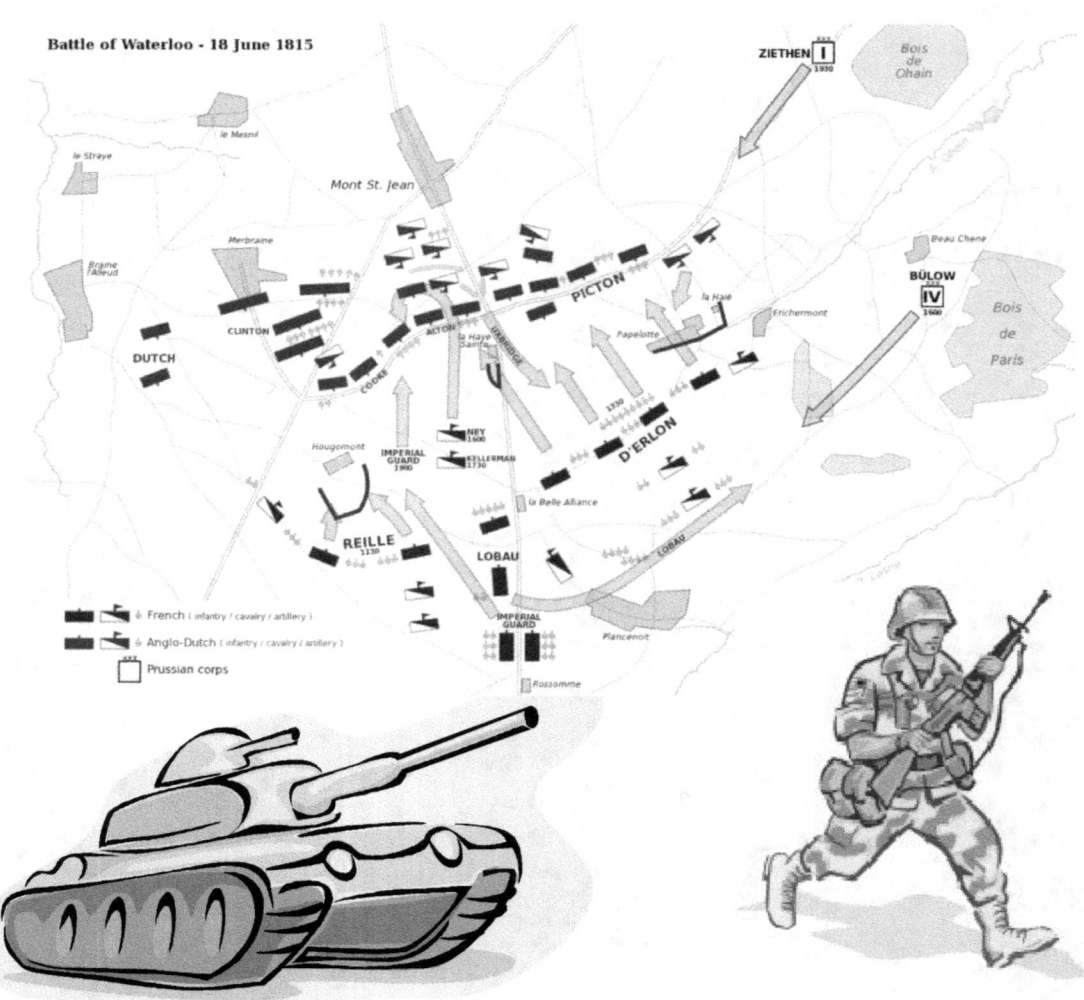

LESSON 5
ONOMATOPOEIA AND INTERJECTIONS

There are many tools to help transform dry writing into a story that is alive. One of those tools is called Onomatopoeia (Pronunciation: ah-nê-mæ-dê-pee-ê). This is a word that creates a sound effect that mimics the thing described, making the description more expressive. These words are fun to say and fun to read! They add sound and excitement to a story and you will love to include them as you write.

Examples: *Boom! Whiz! Splat! Wham!*

- *Boom!* The cannon shook the ground.
- Bullets **whizzed** past him.
- *Kaboom!* The bridge blew up into a million pieces.

Circle 5 Onomatopoeia sounds that make you think of a battlefield. Use them in your story as you write today.

Boom	Crash	Screech
Bang	Crunch	Splat
Bash	Pow	Sploosh
Boink	Gulp	Spray
Blam	Gurgle	Squirt
Crouch	Kaboom	Thump
Clink	Kapow	Whiz
Clap	Roar	Zap

INTERJECTIONS

An interjection is a part of speech that usually comes at the beginning of a sentence to show strong emotion, surprise or excitement. Unlike onomatopoeia words, they don't mimic sound but express emotion. They are usually punctuated with an exclamation point or a comma if the feeling is not as strong.

The word in bold is the interjection.

Examples:

- **Yahoo!** We won!
- **Whoa!** That's a big army.
- **Grrr!** This back pack is heavy.

Circle 5 interjections below that you could use in your story.

Ah	Gee	Shhh
Awe	Hey, Hi, Hello	Vroom
Bingo	Hurray	Well
Boo	Oh-Oh	Wow
Bravo	Ok	Whoa
Bye	Ouch	Whoops
Eek	Phew	Yahoo
Fiddlesticks	Rats	Yippee

PRACTICE WRITING INTERJECTIONS AS COMICS.

WRITING TIME - Continue your story by writing several paragraphs using your plot outline for day 2. Skip every other line so you can add things in later. If you need more writing pages, look in the back of this book.

BATTLE CRAFT
MAKE A CLAY DIORAMA OF THE BATTLE FIELD

Get an Adult's Help to make Homemade Clay

Combine:

2 cups flour
1 cup salt
4 teaspoons of cream of tartar

Add:
2 cups of water
2 tablespoons of oil

Cook together on medium heat stirring constantly until a ball is formed. It may look like a goopy mess at first, but persevere! Put on a non stick surface until it's cool enough to touch. Knead until smooth.

Shape clay for buildings, tree trunks, fallen logs, hills, cars, etc. Bake in 200 degree oven for 10 – 40 minutes until clay hardens. Bigger and thicker objects will take longer. Let cool. Then paint.

Take a large shirt box. Glue an 11 x 14 piece of green or brown construction paper to the bottom of the box to form the ground, grass and dirt of your battlefield. Use blue paper for lakes, rivers, etc.

Place items where you want them in the box.

Bring out your tiny army men or buy some at the dollar store. Arrange them in your diorama.

LESSON 6
PERSONIFICATION

Personification is giving person-like qualities to non-living things. Like: The bullets danced around his head or fear wrapped its strong arms around his waist and squeezed. Bullets can't really dance and fear has no arms but it gives a word picture of the story and makes it more exciting! On the lines below write a sentence giving each word human qualities.

Courage
_____
_____
_____

Happiness
_____
_____
_____

Excitement
_____
_____
_____

Fear
_____
_____
_____

Sorrow
_____
_____
_____

WRITING TIME - Continue your story by writing several paragraphs using your plot outline for day 3. Skip every other line so you can add things in later.

BATTLE ACTIVITY - Draw a picture of your character below and color it. Put it in your folder to use in your book when you put it all together later on. On the following pages are ideas to help you.

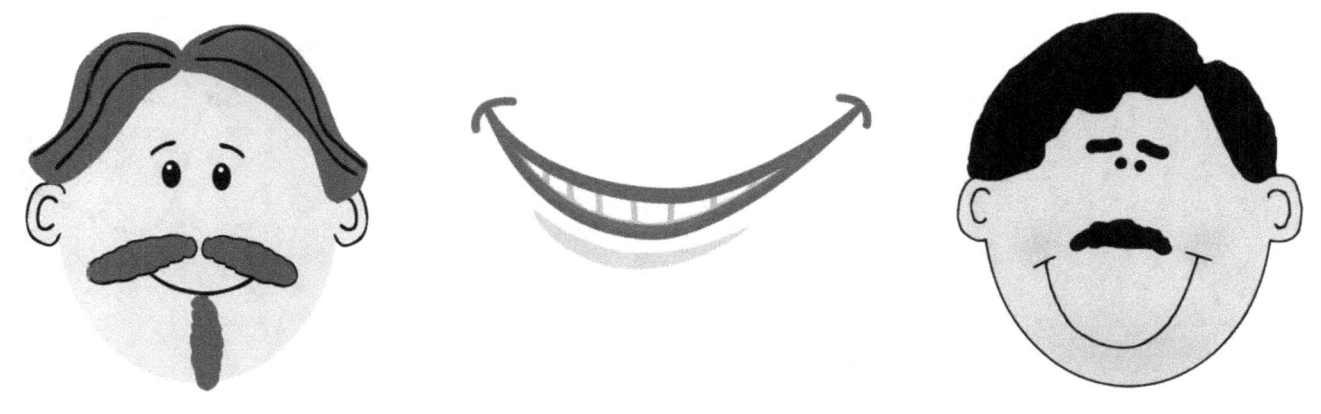

LESSON 7
SIMILES

USING COMPARISONS WITH SIMILES

A simile is a way to compare one thing to another by using the words like or as. It helps to paint a picture of your story with words. Fill in the lines below:

Your character is as tall as _____

He runs like_____

He is strong as _____

On his birthday he is happy as_____

The sun is as hot as _____

Using animal comparisons are fun too! See if you can use animals in the comparisons below:

He laughs like a _____

He moves as slow as a _____

He was as hungry as _____

He fought like a _____

Read the next two pages about animals in warfare. As you continue writing think about including some animals in your battle story.

ANIMALS IN THE MILITARY

Dolphins

The Marine Mammal Program of the U.S. Navy started in 1960. The program was started to study dolphins and beluga whales in order to design more efficient methods of detecting objects underwater. The dolphins could find mines and the humans could dispose them, with the dolphins safely away from the area.

The M.M.P. also studied how dolphins swam in order to develop their boats and submarines to move faster and plunge deeper underwater. Dolphins are amazing because they can dive over and over again without getting decompression sickness like humans: a condition where the rapid water pressure change forms nitrogen bubbles in the blood when divers go down or up in the water too quickly. This can cause pain, visual problems, dizziness and in severe cases, paralysis.

During the Vietnam and Persian Gulf Wars, enemy swimmers would secretly try to climb aboard ships and plant explosives. Bottlenose dolphins were trained to use their echolocation: an ability to sense an object's size, shape and speed hundreds of yards away in the water. Then they would alert the trainers of the intruders! The dolphins could also tag the enemy swimmer with a marker so that the Navy could find them and catch them. In other instances bottlenose dolphins used their echolocation to detect and mark underwater mines by depositing a weighed buoy line near the mines to mark its location.

In 2003 the Persian Gulf was cleared of mines by two dolphins: K-Dog and Katrina so a coalition of U.S. vessels could get to Iraq. They worked with humans for three days to clear the shipping lanes recovering 90 mines and destroyed 11 mines in the waterway. The team cleared 913 marine miles of water space with not one casualty.

ANIMALS IN THE MILITARY

Dogs have been used in warfare since ancient times. Special breeds were trained for the purpose of war, such as the extinct Molossus of the ancient region of Epirus, Greece. These dogs were a large breed similar to today's Mastiffs which weigh 150-200 pounds. There are stories of these dogs wearing spikes around their necks and chainmail armor in battle. Greeks, Romans, and even Attila the Hun used Molossus. Wolfhounds weighing 150-180 pounds were also used in medieval times to bring down the Norman Knights on horseback by the defending Irish.

It was very common in early history that war dogs were given to royalty as a gift. In 1525, King Henry VIII shipped 400 mastiffs out to Spain, as a gift to the Holy Roman Emperor Charles V to support him in his wars against France.

The uses of dogs in modern warfare drastically changed when firearms and long distance weapons were invented. Hand to hand combat was no longer the common form of fighting. The use of dogs soon changed to being message carriers, guards or patrollers.

After the attack on Pearl Harbor in December 1941, the U.S. Military established Dogs for Defense (DFD). German submarines crept closer to U.S. Atlantic and Gulf shores and guard dogs were just what they needed to alert the Navy!

With the word out that dogs were needed to help in the war effort, many patriotic families volunteered their dogs for the new K-9 Corps. This is where Chips, the heroic Shepherd-mix from Pleasantville, New York was discovered. He was a quick learner and served bravely as a tank guard dog. He traveled with General Patton's Seventh Army to

Europe, Africa and Italy. One morning on a beach in Sicily, Chips and his handler discovered a hidden pillbox: an enemy concrete fort with holes for windows to shoot weapons from. The enemy fired on them and Chips broke free and bravely launched himself right into the pillbox. Moments later several bitten Italian soldiers ran out to surrender! Later that night Chips returned to camp wounded and alerted the troops that more Italians were approaching. Because of the alert the squad had time to capture them all.

Chips was awarded a Silver Star for valor and a Purple Heart for his wounds, however the Commander of the Order of the Purple Heart complained that it demeaned the two footed human soldiers so no military dog has received an official decoration since. The brave dog was honorably discharged and returned to his family in Pleasantville.

Today in 2017, there are special awards given to dogs in the military like the Louis Pope LIFE K-9 Medal of Courage. Also many soldiers who are awarded purple hearts will share their awards in an honorary way with their canine battled buddies.

BATTLE ACTIVITY
Can you think of ways the military could use other kinds of animals? On the next page fill out the Top Secret Military file for animals to help in warfare. Under each picture write a job that they can do.

T

TOP SECRET MILITARY FILE FOR ANIMALS IN WARFARE

_____

_____

_____

_____

_____

_____

WRITING TIME - Continue your story by writing several paragraphs using your plot outline for day 4. Skip every other line so you can add things in later.

LESSON 8
"SHOW, DON'T TELL"

C.S. Lewis, author of the popular Chronicles of Narnia series, once said, "In writing, don't merely tell us how you want us to feel. . . I mean, instead of telling us a thing was "terrible," describe it so that we'll be terrified. Don't say it was "delightful"; make us say "delightful" when we've read the description."

A good story describes the body language when a character is emotional making the story come alive. This is the Golden Rule of Writing called "Show, Don't Tell."

Here are two examples of someone who is afraid:

1. **These sentences TELL me he is afraid:**
   GI Joe crept into the abandoned building and he heard a sound. He was afraid.

2. **These sentences SHOW me his body language when he is afraid:**
   GI Joe crept into the abandoned building and he heard a sound. His heart pounded like a drum. Sweat beaded on his forehead as he wrapped his finger around the cold metal of his M16.

Can you feel G.I. Joe's emotions better in the second sentence? Can you see them, too? Now, you try. Turn to the next page and fill in the blanks.

PRACTICE "SHOWING NOT TELLING"

A person's facial expression and how they move their body is called body language. They don't even have to say a word; you can SEE what they are feeling. What would a person LOOK LIKE if they experienced each of these things? You can use more than one sentence.

Excitement
_____
_____

Fear
_____
_____

Anger
_____
_____

BATTLE ACTIVITY
BUILD A FORT FOR INSPIRATION

Take a long rope and tie the ends to opposite sides of the room. Hang a large sheet over the rope and put chairs on the ends to fan the tent out. Lay heavy books on the chairs to keep the sheet in place. Add pillows and blankets inside to make it cozy. Bring in your favorite soldier books. Bring any plastic army men you have inside the fort and role-play your story. Write down any new ideas that you get for your story in your battle book.

WRITING TIME - Continue your story by writing several paragraphs using your plot outline for day 5. Skip every other line so you can add things in later.

LESSON 9
MAKE THE MOST OF DIALOGUE

Dialogue is when a person in your story is talking. Use quotation marks when your characters start to talk and at the end, when they are finished. Put all ending punctuation marks, like periods, inside of the quotation marks.

Example: "Joe, how much ammunition do we have left?" asked Sergeant Malone.

Good dialogue adds interest and action to a story. Sometimes when you have a lot of information you want to tell, you can do it easier using dialogue. Answers are on page 96.

1. **Dialogue can give information about the character. Example:**

"Kyle, why do you always chew gum and bounce your leg up and down?" said Joe. What does this tell about Kyle?

_____

2. **Dialogue can give information about the setting. Example:**

"You two men go over by the empty building," instructed Sergeant Malone. "You three keep the people off the streets." What does this tell about where they are?

_____

STAGE DIRECTIONS

Another way to spice up your dialogue is to "fill in" some details about what the person is doing while they are talking. It's like in a play when the actors are told what to do while they are speaking. The underlined words are the stage directions.

Example:

"Guard the castle while I am gone!" said Kyle, <u>swinging his pretend sword.</u>

"You run as fast as a cheetah!" exclaimed Private Mullens, <u>sprinting alongside the soldiers.</u>

Remember how we left an empty line between our sentences? Now you have room to add in some important details. Go through your story's dialogue and see if you can "fill in" some of the details about what the characters are doing as they are talking. You can write it in the line above the quote. Try to "fill in" details with only about half of your lines of dialogue in your story, adding details to every line would be too much.

BATTLE ACTIVITY

Role-play your story by inviting friends over for a Nerf or water gun war in your back yard.

TAG LINES

After a line of dialogue we add what's called a tag line. It's that part of the sentence that tells who said it. For example:

"Incoming fire!" yelled GI Joe. Yelled GI Joe is the tag line. You could write: said GI Joe, but it wouldn't be as exciting or express the mood of the battle as well as yelled GI Joe.

There are tons of ways to write a tag line instead of using the word said. Below is a list of many. You can even add your own. Circle 10 words you like and use them somewhere in your story. Go back and see if you can replace some "saids" with the words below.

added	comforted	implied	pleaded
admitted	complained	informed	praised
agreed	confessed	insisted	prayed
announced	coughed	insulted	preached
avowed	cried	jabbered	predicted
barked	croaked	jested	protested
begged	defended	joked	quarreled
blew up	denied	judged	questioned
boasted	echoed	laughed	raged
bragged	gagged	lied	railed
breathed	grunted	mimicked	screamed
called	gulped	moaned	screeched
cautioned	gurgled	muttered	scoffed
challenged	gushed	nagged	scolded
cheered	hesitated	ordered	shouted
chided	hissed	persisted	shrieked
choked	hooted	pestered	teased
chuckled	howled	petitioned	yelled

WRITING TIME - Continue your story by writing several paragraphs using your plot outline for day 6. Skip every other line so you can add things in later.

LESSON 10
ADD AN ADJECTIVE

It's time to spice up your story. Adding adjectives to the nouns in your story helps to create a picture in the mind of the reader. It's like starting your story in black and white then switching on the color. This also helps the reader to experience your story, not just read it.

A noun is a person, place, or thing.

An adjective is a word used to describe a noun. It can tell which one, what kind, how many, what color, or what texture.

Add an adjective in each of the blanks below for practice:

1. The _____ rain made it hard for the men to see what was ahead.

2. GI Joe saw the _____ smoke rising from the _____ building.

3. The _____ squad of soldiers trudged across the _____ field.

4. GI Joe put on his _____ boots for his _____ work day on the base.

5. GI Joe's _____ drill sergeant, called his name.

Go over your story now and add an adjective to a noun in every other sentence.

WRITING TIME - Continue your story by writing several paragraphs using your plot outline for day 7 and 8. Skip every other line so you can add things in later.

BATTLE CRAFT
CAMOUFLAGE MARBLE PAINTED TANK

YOU WILL NEED:

- Shallow shirt box – 9 x 11
- Acrylic paints in camouflage colors: tan, green, and brown
- Marbles
- Tan, white, or light green piece of construction paper

DIRECTIONS:

- IMPORTANT: Read all instructions before you begin!
- Tape down your piece of construction paper inside the bottom center of the box.
  Carefully cut out the tank image on next page and set the tank aside. Don't crumble up the outer paper-this is what you will use for this project. You should be able to see a cut out shape in the middle of the tank paper.
- Tape the white cut-away part of the tank inside the box, on top of the construction paper.
- Squirt the 3 different colors of paint around the edges several times
- Drop several marbles inside the box and roll them around by picking up the box and shifting it around. You will create a camouflage marbled affect shaped like a tank on the paper.
- Let dry. Gently peel off tape and white cut-out paper.
- Add picture to your folder or mount on larger construction paper.

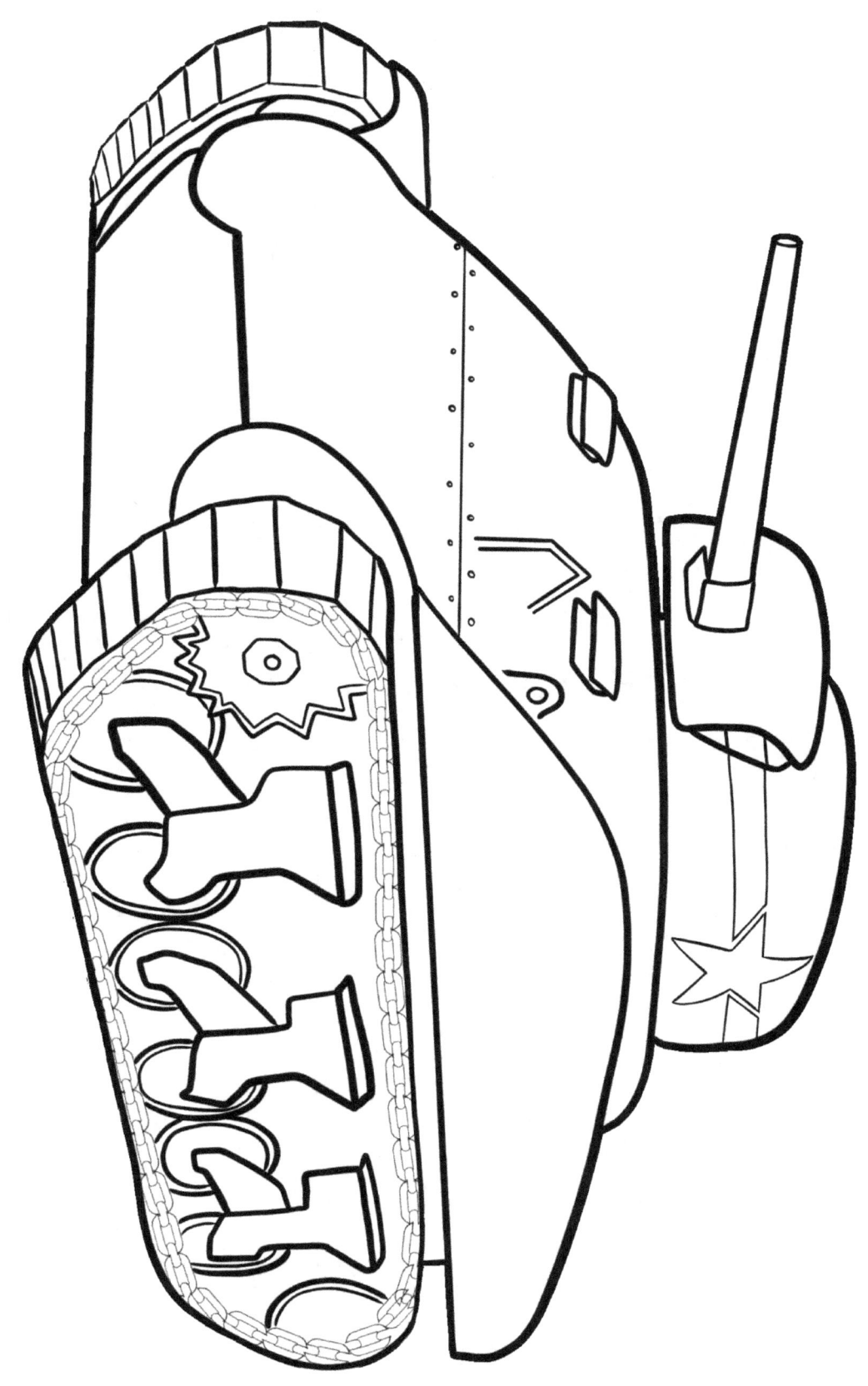

LESSON 11
STRONG VERBS

All verbs show action but all verbs are not the same in strength. Wow Words are verbs that show a picture of what is going on and gives your story punch. Weak verbs are over used and wimpy. They don't show much of anything.

For example, you could say: "GI Joe ran across the field."

The verb is ran. If he was in a hurry, you could say, he darted or bolted across the field. These words add more punch.

A thesaurus is a helpful book of synonyms. It lists words that are similar to each other.

Using a thesaurus, look up each word below and write two stronger ways to write each word:

Fell _____ _____

Walk _____ _____

Carry _____ _____

Limp _____ _____

Crawl _____ _____

The word **went** is a also a very weak verb. Try to use it as least as possible. On the next page are words to use instead of went. **Circle 10 words from** the list and see if you can change any "wents" in your story and replace them with the circled words.

STRONGER WAYS TO SAY WENT

Advanced	Fell	Rambled
Ambled	Flew	Retreated
Approached	Flitted	Roamed
Ascended	Floated	Rocketed
Barreled	Followed	Rushed
Blasted	Glided	Sailed
Bolted	Groveled	Scrambled
Boogied	Hastened	Scuttled
Bounced	Hightailed	Slithered
Bounded	Hiked	Staggered
Burst	Hoofed it	Stormed
Chugged	Hopped	Stumbled
Climbed	Hurdled	Traipsed
Crawled	Hurried	Vanished
Crept	Inched	Ventured
Cruised	Journeyed	Waddled
Danced	Loped	Wafted
Darted	Marched	Whisked
Dashed	Nosed	Withdrew
Encroached	Pounced	Wormed
Entered	Pushed on	Zipped
Escaped	Raced	Zoomed

WRITING TIME - Finish your story using your plot outline for days 9 and 10. Skip every other line so you can add things in later.

BATTLE ACTIVITY

On a piece of white paper draw a scene from your story and color it. Put it in your battle folder to use when you put together your story once you are finished.

LESSON 12
EDITING

To edit or revise something means to correct any mistakes and change things to make it better. Many great writers revise their stories ten to twenty times! We will only do it once. Here is a check list to help:

_____1. Check your spelling and have a parent check too. Reading your story out loud helps to catch errors. Use spell check if you are typing on a computer.

_____2. Check that every sentence begins with a capital letter and ends with a period, question mark or exclamation point.

_____3. Can you combine any two smaller sentences and make them into a bigger sentence? For example: Jack is tall. Jack runs fast. To combine: Jack is tall and runs fast.

_____4. Are all the punctuation marks of your dialogue *inside* the quotation marks?

_____5. Have you used all five senses in describing the setting somewhere in your story? Check them off below as you find them or add some in.
- Sights _____
- Sounds _____
- Tastes _____
- Textures_____
- Smells _____

_____ 6. After you have checked off all of the above, you can neatly rewrite your story with all the corrections on it. You can use the lined paper in the back of the book or type it out on the computer.

PUTTING IT ALL TOGETHER

Draw and color a title page or fill out the ready-made title page on the next page.

Number all your final story pages. Arrange them by putting all drawings and maps in the right places. Three-hole punch all the pages then put them into a plastic essay binder along with your title page. The essay binders can be found at a superstore or office supply store.

BATTLE ACTIVITY
FLASHLIGHT THEATRE & CAPTURE THE FLAG PARTY

Turn all the lights out in a room and flash several flashlights on the reader as each student reads their stories. The students can sit at a table, on a living room chair, or in a tent with a flashlight shining on their story. Imitate battle sounds as you read for a realistic effect. For fun, dress up in military gear and cut out a large square in a big box and make a TV. Paint it in camouflage colors then read behind it after it's dry. Remember to follow good flashlight behavior: No flashing in anyone's eyes or waving lights around to make fun patterns on the wall. Invite friends, grandparents, cousins, or other families to be in the audience. Make popcorn or other fun snacks found on the next page to share! ☺

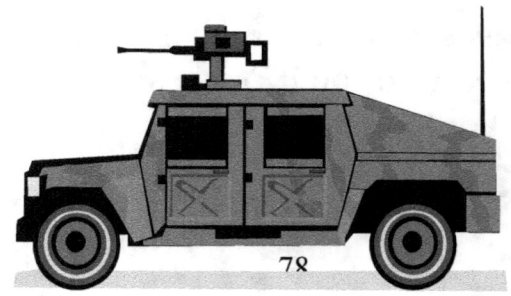

BATTLE FLASHLIGHT THEATER & CAPTURE THE FLAG PARTY

MAKE YOUR OWN MRE SNACK MIX

Set out 10 different snack items in bowels. Let each person add a scoop of their favorite snack into a plastic sandwich bag and shake them together!

Salty Snacks

- Small cheese crackers
- Cheese or plain popcorn
- Pretzels, plain or chocolate covered
- Corn chips
- Gluten free crackers
- Nuts – watch for allergies!
- Tiny peanut butter or cheese filled crackers
- Sunflower seeds

Sweet Snacks

- Chocolate chips
- Butterscotch chips
- Brownie or cookie pieces
- Tiny cookies in favorite flavors
- Caramel popcorn
- Marshmallows
- Raisins
- Dried fruits-apricots or cherries cut up
- Favorite crunchy sweet cereal balls, puffs, or squares

HOW TO PLAY CAPTURE THE FLAG

Two teams hide a flag on their territory. Mark the territory by dividing a playing area in half with trees, bushes, cones, sticks or other markers. Each team tries to be the first to capture the opponents' flag and bring it back to their territory. To defend your team's flag, tag opponents found on your territory and send them to "jail" until they are tagged by their teammate to be set free. The first team to capture the other's flag wins the round. To play at night dress in dark colors.

For more ideas for fun military party games visit our Pintrest Page: https://www.pinterest.com/janmay2012/military-party-ideas-for-boys/

_____

By

_____

MODERN WEAPONS AND ARTILLERY

GEAR
Rucksack - to hold all gear
Night Goggles
Helmet - Does it have a mounted technical screen?
Smartphone, GPS, tablet
Parachute
Binoculars
IOTVs (Improved Outer Tactical Vests) provides protection against small arms, shrapnel and debris
Advanced Combat Optical Gunsight

WEAPONS
M16 Assault Rifle
M16 Grenade Launcher
Javelin Anti -Tank Missile
50 Cal Machine Gun
M777 Howitzer
Missile Launchers
Cluster Bombs
Missile Anti-Tank Mines
Rockets
Grenades

VEHICLES
Blackhawk Helicopter
MrapTank-M 1 Abrams (Mine-Resistant Ambush Protected) against explosives
Armored Personnel Carrier Tanks
- Stryker
- Grizzly
- Rhino Runner
- Amphibious Assault Vehicle

LIGHT ARMORED VEHICLES

- Gun truck
- Wiesel
- Ambulance
- Dessert Patrol Vehicle

MINE PROTECTED VEHICLES

- Buffalo 200
- Cougar 3,500
- Casspir
- RG 31

COMBAT

- M9 Armored Combat Earthmover
- Caterpillar D 7
- M 104 Wolverine Armored Bridge Layer
- M88 Recovery Vehicle- Recovers damaged vehicles from the frontline

SELF-PROPELLED ARTILLERY AND AIR DEFENSE

- M 6 Linebacker
- Stryker Mobile Gun System
- Dragon Fire
- Avenger
- Patriot

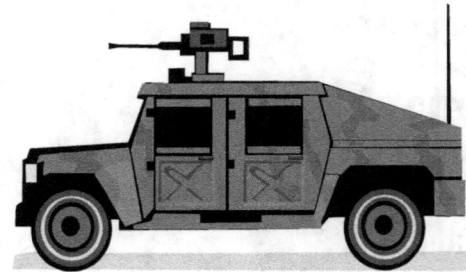

UNMANNED COMBAT VEHICLES

- Dragon Runner
- Black Knight
- Armed Robotic Vehicle

U.S. ARMY MILITARY ORGANIZATION DEFINITIONS:

FIRE TEAM: Made up of 2 Riflemen, one being the Team Leader, a Grenadier (a soldier armed with grenades or a grenade launcher), and an Automatic Rifleman.

SQUAD/SECTION: This is the smallest unit of soldiers made up of 4 to 10 soldiers commanded by a **sergeant**.

PLATOON: Includes 16 to 44 soldiers led by a lieutenant and usually consists of 3 to 4 squads or sections.

COMPANY: A company contains 3 to 5 platoons and a total of 60 to 200 soldiers. It's commanded by a **captain**. If the company is an artillery unit, it's called a battery. If it's armored or air cavalry, it's called a troop.

BATTALION: Made up of 4 to 6 companies and between 300 and 1,000 soldiers. It is commanded by a **lieutenant colonel**. A battalion can conduct independent operations.

BRIGADE: A brigade includes 1,500 to 3,200 soldiers, and the brigade headquarters commands the tactical operation of 2 to 5 combat battalions. It is commanded by sergeant major or a brigadier general.

DIVISION: A division, with 10,000 to 16,000 soldiers, usually consists of 3 brigades and is commanded by a **major general**, who is assisted by two brigadier generals. It can conduct major tactical and battlefield operations.

CORPS: A corps includes 20,000 to 45,000 soldiers and is made up of 2 to 5 divisions. It's commanded by a lieutenant general and has an extensive corps staff. The corps provides the structure for modern multi-national operations.

FIELD ARMY: A field army combines 2 or more corps, with 50,000 or more soldiers, and is commanded by a lieutenant general or higher-ranking officer. This army group plans and **directs** large scale operations for specific goals.

https://www.thebalancecareers.com/u-s-army-military-organization-from-squad-to-corps-

U.S. MILITARY RANKS

Rank means position. From a beginner soldier who is a Private to the Five- Star General who is in charge of everything, there are a lot of ranks in the military! The lists below start from lowest ranking positions to the highest. This is not a complete list but a few ranks from each division to stir your imagination!

ARMY: Private, Corporal, Sergeant, Captain, Major, Lieutenant, Colonel, Brigadier General, Five- Star General of the Army

MARINE CORPS: Private, Private First Class, Corporal, Sergeant, Gunnery Sergeant, Master Sergeant

AIR FORCE: Airman, Staff Sergeant, Master Sergeant, Lieutenant, Captain, Major, Colonel, Brigadier General, Five- Star General of Air Force

NAVY: Seaman, Petty Officer, Ensign, Lieutenant, Commander, Captain, Admiral

ANSWERS FOR PAGE 32

1. Get Pizza
2. Play Outside
3. Bake Cookies with Me

ANSWERS FOR PAGE 64

1. This tells us that Kyle is nervous
2. This tells us they are in a city

*The U.S. Military alphabet code for W is Whiskey but has been changed to Walrus to make it appropriate for children.

ABOUT THE AUTHOR

Jan May loved homeschooling her two children through high school. Whether it was attending re-enactments of the Revolutionary War or collecting an amphibian zoo, hands-on education was always at the forefront of her curriculum. She is author of the *Creative Writing Made Easy* series that engages even the most reluctant writers. All of the books are filled with fun interactive language activities involving each type of learner: visual, auditory and kinesthetic- perfect for the wiggle in boys. Having been a creative writing teacher for over fifteen years, she believes that given the right tools, every child can learn to write and love it!

Visit her website for fun battle downloads and activities. Watch for her online teaching schedule- leading students and teens in a fun and engaging writing experience! www.NewMillenniumGirlBooks.com

If you like this book, you might also enjoy ***Spies of the Revolutionary War Writing Unit***. It makes learning fun and includes a lapbbok! Order this book and more at www.NewMillenniumGirlBooks.com

- Learn about the minutemen and the spies of the Revolutionary War
- Make a battle drum, create your own secret code, and make a dead drop secret message carrier
- Memorize parts of Patrick Henry's famous speech: *Give me Liberty or Give me Death!*
- Become a spy character and write about it.
- Read the famous poem "Paul Revere's Ride"
- Role-play your stories!

www.ingramcontent.com/pod-product-compliance
Lightning Source LLC
Chambersburg PA
CBHW051419070526
44584CB00023B/3501